D1504976

"HONESTY IS ONE OF THE *BETTER* POLICIES"

"HONESTY IS ONE OF THE BETTER POLICIES"

Saxon's
WORLD OF BUSINESS

THE VIKING PRESS   NEW YORK

The Introduction to this book is an expanded version of the article
"How to Draw a Businessman," which appeared originally in *The New York Times.*

Library of Congress Cataloging in Publication Data
Saxon, Charles D.
"Honesty is one of the *better* policies."
1. Business—Caricatures and cartoons.
2. American wit and humor, Pictorial.   I. Title.
NC1429.S35A4   1984   741.5'973   83-47979
ISBN 0-670-19753-X

Acknowledgment is made to the following, who originally published some of the cartoons in this
book, and to those who have retained copyright, for permission to reprint: *Architectural Record*;
cartoons on pages 49, 74, courtesy Bank of New England; cartoon on page 84, courtesy California
Casualty Insurance Group; *One Man's Fancy* by Charles Saxon, Copyright © 1977 by Charles Saxon,
Dodd, Mead & Company, Inc.; cartoon on page 16, Copyright © Eastman Kodak Company, 1978;
cartoon on page 17, Copyright © Eastman Kodak Company, 1978; cartoon on page 22, Copyright
© Eastman Kodak Company, 1981; cartoon on page 12, Fairchild Publications; *Forbes*; cartoon on
page 37, courtesy Ford Financial Services, Inc.; *Fortune* magazine; cartoon on page 47, courtesy
Las Vegas Convention and Visitors Authority; cartoon on page 27, courtesy *New England Business*
magazine; cartoons on pages 26, 28, *The New York Times*, Copyright © The New York Times
Company; *Newsweek*; cartoon on page 24, *Playboy* magazine, Copyright © 1975 by Playboy;
cartoon on page 25, courtesy Price Waterhouse; cartoon on page 65, *Punch* magazine, Rothco
Cartoons, Inc., Copyright © 1964 by Punch; *Town & Country* magazine; cartoon on page 23,
Chicago Tribune, courtesy Tribune Company Syndicate, Inc.

Thirty-nine of the cartoons in this collection first appeared in *The New Yorker.* Copyright
© 1967, 1968, 1970, 1971, 1972, 1973, 1974, 1975, 1977, 1978, 1979, 1980, 1981, 1982 by
The New Yorker, Inc.

Printed in the United States of America
Set in Linotron Zapf Light International

For Amanda, Rogers and Peter

with love

Introduction

I like to draw businessmen. Living in one of New York's commuter suburbs, it was natural that I would find sources of humor among the people I live with. Some of my best friends are businessmen. When I started drawing for *The New Yorker*, the late art director James Geraghty studied my pictures with a puzzled look. "All your people look like stockbrokers," he said. "I think if you were drawing Yugoslavian fishermen they'd look like stockbrokers with nets."

Other characters have certainly found their way into my drawings but, with a bow to my editor and dear friend, this book is focused on stockbrokers and their ilk.

Obviously there are many subcategories of businessmen. Some are young, some old. Some clerk in the stockroom, others are chairmen of the boards. In recent years there has been an emergence of women, blacks, and so-called ethnic groups in the office, but more on them later. The symbolic prototype is the middle-aged club-type executive.

As I visualize him I don't see a stock caricature. I don't find him a ridiculous figure. Rather, he is an average man, like anybody else, but by chance and considerable effort he finds himself a bureaucrat. Perhaps he dreamed of being an archaeologist in his undergraduate days, or a tennis pro. Maybe he flunked out of a premed course or had to leave college to get a job when his family went broke. Maybe he never went to college at all and worked his way up from being a shipping clerk. However it happened, here he sits behind a big desk with a push-button telephone, in an office with a corner window: a pillar of the Establishment, maker of decisions, symbol of power.

But he isn't all that secure, really. He's probably overextended at the bank. He secretly questions his status, worries over whether he is measuring up to his image. He has built a careful structure to bolster his confidence with the kind of friends he chooses, the place where he lives, the clubs he joins, the clothes he wears, the way he combs his hair. His peers buy the package, but his teenage son makes him uncomfortable.

The executive carries his persona beyond the boardroom, of course. He is unmistakable in swimsuit or jogging togs, on the golf course or among the ruins of Greece. You'll find him on these pages in his fantasy world as well—or is it my fantasy world?

I'm not a sociologist. When I draw, I feel an empathy for this man. I draw him in the role he plays. His Bill Blass suit is a little tight across the middle, but he tries to hold his stomach in and his shoulders back. When he's on his stage, he stands as if he were posing for a photo in *Fortune*. His facial expression rarely relaxes. He usually remembers to keep his hands out of his pockets and look composed. The over-all effect is rather pompous. This pomposity is a prime ingredient in the kind of cartoon situation in which my businessmen are found because they take themselves quite seriously, and the humor is revealed in the viewer's perception of this.

The "typical middle-aged executive" is the main character, but the big problem for cartoonists is that most businessmen don't fit the stereotype. People in advertising, communications, and even in ordinary fields of commerce are very likely to defy generalization. So to avoid confusion and make the point quickly we have to forgo offbeat clothes, wild hair, and beards unless the situation specifically demands it. Thank God for bankers, insurance men, and stockbrokers! They *always* comb their hair and wear ties.

Today women, blacks, and all ethnic groups are part of the executive mainstream. To be really on top of things, half the businessmen I draw should be Japanese. Nevertheless, in spite of the changes, it remains difficult to include women and blacks in normal office cartoons because their presence draws too much attention and the point of the idea get sidetracked. For example, I drew a cartoon of a scene at a library checkout counter. A middle-aged man is embarrassed at being the only adult in a queue of kids. I thought it would be a nice touch to make the female librarian black. The cartoon failed. Everybody missed the point because they were focused on the librarian. I'm pleased to report that many art directors now request the inclusion of blacks and women in office scenes, but

for most cartoons, relaxed assimilation is yet to come.

I get a number of assignments from abroad which have to do with business situations. The art directors obviously chose my style for the characters they were familiar with, but they often want a delicate variation on the familiar without getting ethnic caricatures. One Italian agency sent back a set of my drawings that all featured the same central character. They said the man I had drawn just didn't typify the proper Italian. What they had in mind, they explained, was somebody like Walter Matthau. We compromised.

Most of the drawings in this book first appeared in *The New Yorker*. There is little I can add to all that has been written about *The New Yorker* and its standards of excellence. For a cartoonist, to satisfy its editors represents the ultimate challenge. There are no rules. What they demand is simply the best you have in you.

Drawing for advertising is a different kind of challenge, and conflicts frequently arise about the function of graphic humor. It has been proven by many surveys that a nice, clean ad with lots of white space and a bold cartoon not only gets high readership but also remarkably high reader recall of the product being advertised. Consequently, some industrial advertisers with a deadly, dry story to tell think of using a cartoon to brighten up the message. A message such as, "Our quarterly net has risen fourteen percent." They say, why not have a cartoon of a couple of businessmen doing something funny?

Faced with this problem, I remember two basic rules I have learned. The first: a cartoon, wherever it is used, has to pay off with something intrinsically funny. A cartoon captioned "Our net has risen fourteen percent" is a cheat. The reader has been booby-trapped, and instead of being amused, he is annoyed and the ad fails. The second: humor is a delicate commodity. The appearance of humor doesn't pass for the real thing. Even when used commercially it has to have bite; and a cartoon attempting to eulogize a product is nowhere near as effective as one that takes a swipe at the awful consequences of *not* using the product.

This is as close as I dare come to analyzing humor. As E. B. White said, humor can be dissected, like a frog, but you end up with a dead frog.

The cartoonist's job, of course, is to communicate ideas humorously, but the process of creating cartoons, as with all the visual arts, is intuitive rather than verbal. The way cartoonists see the world and draw people depends on how observant they are about the way we live, think, and behave. Some draw from life, others create their own private world. When asked why he drew such weird-looking women, James Thurber answered, "They look very attractive to my men." I draw businessmen the way I do because that's the best and funniest I know how.

—Charles Saxon

"HONESTY IS ONE OF THE *BETTER* POLICIES"

"Tell me, Wentworth. If you're not being inscrutable, just what are you being?"

"*Have a nice day, dear, and good luck at lunch.*"

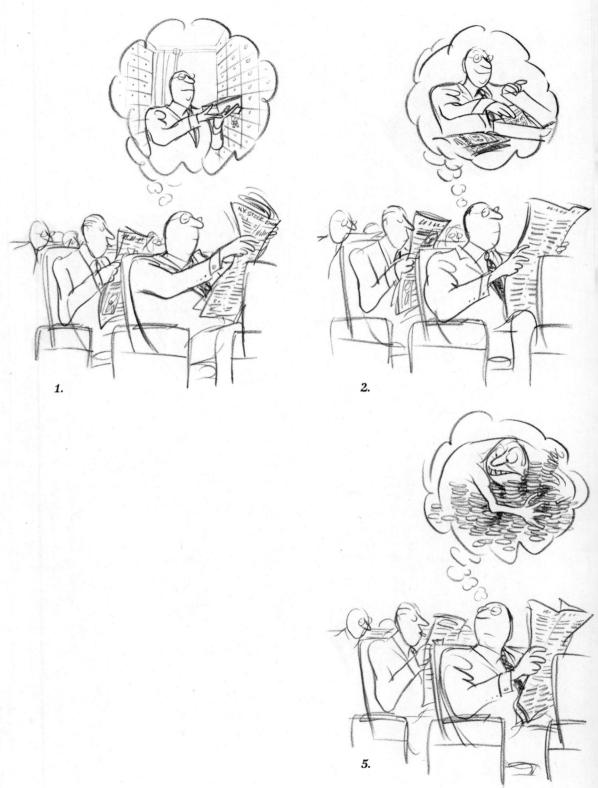

1.

2.

5.

3.

4.

6.

saxon

"If there are any calls, Miss Gilmore, I'll be on the fifteenth floor,
breathing down some necks."

"Oh, that's Helga—the chick who shares my pad."

"I abstain, because of misgivings."

"Tell me, Mr. Wallberg—what in particular can you offer this firm with your so-called youth?"

"Of course, honesty is one of the better policies."

*"Thank you, gentlemen. Although I'm resigning from this board,
my thoughts will be with you. I intend to spend much of my time
relaxing and painting, and my work will be shown at the Forbush Gallery,
East Sixty-eighth Street, just off Park."*

*"Aside from having a lot of experience throwing your weight around,
what have you done?"*

"*I have here six copies . . . six copies of* what, *Mr. Osgood?*"

"*I'm not going to ask who collated and who stapled, but page 43
seems to be someone's letter to her mother in Sarasota.*"

The Fountain of Youth

Of late, Arnold Flagler had begun to spend much of his weekend time walking alone in the woods. One day, he found himself on an unfamiliar path that led him to a small pond.

As he stood beside the pond, the water began to stir and bubbles to rise

until they formed a lovely little fountain, and a voice called, "Arnold Flagler, this is the fountain of youth!"

Mr. Flagler shrank back in fear.
The fountain leaped and soared, and a
sound of unbelievable music filled the air.

"I mean, how does it work? How young will I be?"
The fountain swirled and sang as it danced higher
and higher. "Youth will be yours," it repeated.

The voice called again. "This is the
fountain of youth, Arnold Flagler! Drink!"
"What will happen to me if I drink?" Mr. Flagler asked.
"Youth will be yours," said the fountain.

"Will my family know me?
What about my pension and the cumulative
profit-sharing plan, and all that?"
The voice of the fountain was fainter now.
"Youth will be yours," it said.

"Listen," said Mr. Flagler desperately.
"Just tell me one thing. Has anybody else tried this?
Anybody I know?" The music faded away and the water subsided
until the fountain vanished and the pond was still.

20

Mr. Flagler walked slowly home.

*"What did you do in the woods today?" asked his wife
that evening. "I got lost," said Mr. Flagler.*

21

"*Good news, J.B.! I think this will solve our copier collating problems!*"

*"Perhaps I should explain my concept
behind the term 'good offer.'"*

*"I just realized something!
This same discussion cropped up
in* The Dialogues of Plato!*"*

"Of course, Albuquerque isn't New York, but we try to keep up with things."

Women at the Top

Assault of the women on Chauvinist Heights.

The decline and fall of the all-male business club.

Collisions in the corridors of power.

The chevalier.

The stay-at-homebody.

The last male bastion . . .

meets the new order.

"*Just an informal dinner at home. Put it on my expense account.*"

"I happen to feel a Maserati is therapy."

Perks.

"I'd like to find out who told Forbes
I was a nervous bear."

"I should get back early.
I'm supposed to be on the warpath."

"Today, gentlemen, I would recommend the Trout Almondine,
Veal Cordon Bleu, or if you need a broker . . ."

Sales Conference

*"Gentlemen—we have just missed the
entire round table on Midwest Marketing."*

*"However, current research shows that applying the want-to-buy factor
to the word-of-mouth factor indicates a sharp rise and a great year ahead."*

*"Mr. Fine, Mr. Larraby, and Mr. Reinhardt
are all playing tennis."*

"Drink, Señor?"

"You know what would be a great idea
and save a lot of money? Move the
corporate headquarters to Barbados!"

"Can you make a martini?"

The string tournament.

"Is he one of ours?"

"Turn up the air conditioning and shut the damn bar."

"Lousy weather we're having."

"*I'm here to listen and learn, Mr. Parker, but I warn you—
my father always said never trust a smart-aleck Princeton man.*"

"You've got character, Jennings. And I happen to think that's not a bad thing to have."

"I've asked our Mr. Mackenzie, here, to tuck you into some comfortable trust funds."

"I suggest you take your proposition to Mr. Hotchkiss at the office. He may send you to Sam Watson or Bob Exum. Eventually, of course, you will have to talk to me."

"That's where Daddy's new office will be. In the top left-hand drawer."

The Trip

*Driving back to Hartford
one summer day, not on 90 but the back way
through Claggett's Bridge, Grayson Thomas
was tense at the wheel.*

*He hadn't written up a single policy
on the entire swing through Pittsfield,
but the still, sultry afternoon seemed to be
calling him. There was plenty of time.
Mr. Thomas pulled off the road and stopped.*

Below him, overlooking the Naugatuck Valley, was a small grove of birches, and he walked down through the waving grasses, sat under the flickering shadows of the branches, and closed his eyes. Softly, so softly he was barely surprised to discover he was not alone, a voice asked, *"Tell me of your quest, please."*

"Quest?" said Mr. Thomas. *"Quest? I sell insurance."*

Then he opened his eyes. Sitting beside him was a gossamer figure, translucent in the golden summer light. She was beautiful. "A seller of insurance!" she repeated in a mellifluous, lilting voice. "Oh, what wonderful secrets you must know!"

"Actuarial tables are what I know," said Mr. Thomas. "Life expectancy. Accident risks. Incidence of arson." He sighed. She drew back in awe. "Life! Death! The future! How great is the knowledge of your tables!" she cried.

"Male children born today will live to be sixty-nine," said Mr. Thomas, in spite of himself. "Teenage boys will probably have an automobile accident of some kind."

She sank to the earth on her knees and took his hands.
"Oh, let me come with you and learn your wisdom," she said. "Let me be
with you and be your disciple, your friend. Let me stay by your side under
the stars and hear of the miraculous actuaries who guide you!"

*"I'll tell you what," said Mr. Thomas,
pulling out one of his cards. "Give me a ring at
the office, and maybe we can have lunch.
I've really got to get a move on."*

*Grayson Thomas made it back to
Hartford by four-thirty. He walked purposefully
to his desk and slipped a sheet of paper into
the typewriter. "Expenses of Trip," he wrote.
"Solid prospect, Claggett's Bridge. Disbursements . . ."*

"And where is the quizzical lift of the left eyebrow today, Mr. Griffith?"

"*The market gave a good account of itself today, Daddy, after some mid-morning profit-taking.*"

"First and foremost, of course, it's our hedge against inflation."

"Brian, this is Lars Kronquist. He's a winner, too."

"Naturally you can take the larger view—you've made your pile."

"It's okay if he bakes, or it's okay if he knits. But it's not *okay if he bakes* and *knits.*"

"*There are many forms of creativity, my boy, as you'll discover
if you ever have to draw up a purchase order.*"

"*I assume we're all solvent here, so I'll speak freely.*"

"Pierce, of Bailey, Pierce & Kemp, may I present Archer, of Howe, Archer, Groff & Seaberry."

"When Harold Bigelow said, 'The sky is the daily bread of the eyes,'
all you could come up with was, 'Yes, it's always seemed that way to me, too.'"

"But of course! We always cry during the second act of Tristan."

"I'd expect my doctor to be able to do that,
but not my trust officer!"

"Tell me. Are you having $74,355 worth of fun?"

"Yes, I am going to the club. But I will not be 'hanging out' there."

"What do you say? Shall we get down to some serious bowling?"

Sunday on the links.

"Captain's compliments, sir. The bluefish are running off Nantucket.
Shall we give chase?"

"Well, so far I'd say this vacation
has been a good investment."

"Oh, by the way, dear, where is the key to the safe deposit box?"

"Well, this *should appeal* to you. It's an ancient bill of lading."

"Of course you have a pretty smile. Would I have married a woman with an ugly smile?"

"It's all right, dear. Kidder, Peabody. For me."

"If it's all right with you, I thought we'd do some long-range planning tonight."

"*If you're looking for me, Herbert, I shall be sitting in the bay window reading the Dow Jones summary of corporate earnings.*"

Hang in there!

"I'm writing my autobiography, to set the record straight."

"Why, Clayton, that's not true. You have friends up and down the corporate ladder."

"*Now that you're retiring, you won't be renewing this* Insider's Newsletter, *I assume.*"

Charles Saxon was born in New York City and attended Columbia University. He became a regular contributor to *The New Yorker* in 1956 and his work has also appeared in *Time*, *Newsweek*, *Forbes*, and many other publications. His two previous collections are *Oh, Happy, Happy, Happy* and *One Man's Fancy*. In 1980 Charles Saxon was named Cartoonist of the Year by the National Cartoonists Society.